Acolyte of the Songbird

A Poetry Collection

Tweetie Snow

Dedications

To All the Mothers and Sisters kin to me

Table of Contents

Acolyte of the Songbirds

By Tweetie Snow

Tweet, tweet, tweeting bird

Tweeting bird, I am your loyal admirer,
An acolyte of flight and freedom.
In the sky, I will no longer be a liar,
Humming in the tune of his kingdom.

Hoot, hoot, hooting owl

Wise bird, I am your loyal student,
An acolyte of literature and language.
On the shelf, I will become important.
Hooting the tune of his sublanguage.

Caw, caw, cawing crow

Blackbird, I am your loyal friend,
An acolyte of mischief and madness.
On the wire, I will one day ascend.
Cawing the tune of his sadness.

Coo, coo, cooing dove

Love bird, I am your loyal lover,
An acolyte of peace and patience.
On the branch, I will learn to hover,
Cooing the tune of his renascence.

A Drowning Prince

By Tweetie Snow

Drowning, Drowning,
In a river of endless water.

My head and heart yearn for weightless equanimity,
Under the burden of a crown in my pocket, I hid.
My airless lungs swell with turbulent white rapid,
With breathlessness in water, I create beautiful amity.

Drowning, Drowning,
In a river of bottomless wonders.

My eyes delude visions of halos in the city,
Twinkling torches shine brightly through the fluid.
My throat chokes on the muck and turbid.
I am my own river flowing in perpetual pity.

Drowning, Drowning,
In a river of senseless, weary.

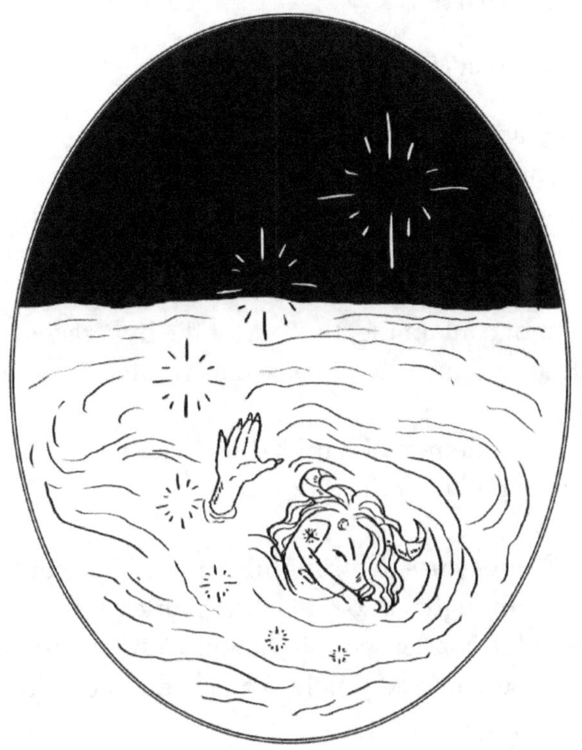

"Drowning, Drowning" by Anonymous Artist

To My Acolytes

By Tweetie Snow

To a drowning prince of nature's angered three,
To a dragon king of death and decay to oversee.

Words pour from the fingers of the emotionally captive,
Worried of the gazing eyes of life's many judges.
Woes cannot contain the illusions of the hyperactive,
Wounds are shamefully disguised as written grudges.

To a timorous demon of damned royal blood,
To a tireless pup of endless hope and mud.

Self-doubt rises lines of wrongfully unworthy chapters,
Sensational thoughts into fantastical stories ever glowing.
Sections of life condensed into fiction without laughter,
Sessions of sorrow and timely vernacular gracefully
flowing.

To a voiceless nightingale painting his feathers,
To a vocal phoenix trapped in stone and weather.

My worlds are encased in the ribcage pumping this soul,
Mystics and wonders rest in the aching and horrid truth.
Mysteries buzz in the consciousness burning like coal.
Mythology stirs the imagination of a withering youth.

To a child with dreams of being an author,
To a chronicle of acolytes waiting on their creator.

A Timorous Demon

By Tweetie Snow

Fire blazes in the stone furnace like Heaven's glow,
The kettle screams in the tone of sharp, sadistic mirth.
No comfort shall a young damned soul know,
Yet all too familiar with a red flame's scorching
warmth.

Across the porch, tread on my toes with a gentle
toddle,
Each patron is allocated to my fate but never my past.
In my father's arms, I am crafted as Hell's faltering
model.

A key lock up shop in a chiming whimper of brittle
bone,
Not a soul left in sight as my hollow chest beats for no
one.
May my father hold me once more, may they bring
me home.

A Tireless Pup

By Tweetie Snow

Pink, blue, and white too.

Sing me a song, little puppy dog,
Have the heart to stand on your stage of innocence.

Glitter, ribbons, soured booze.

Sing me a tune, little puppy dog,
Have the guts to stand on your stage of memories

Rabbits, wolves, missed cues.

Sing me a snatch, little puppy dog,
Have the soul to stand on your stage of winter wind.

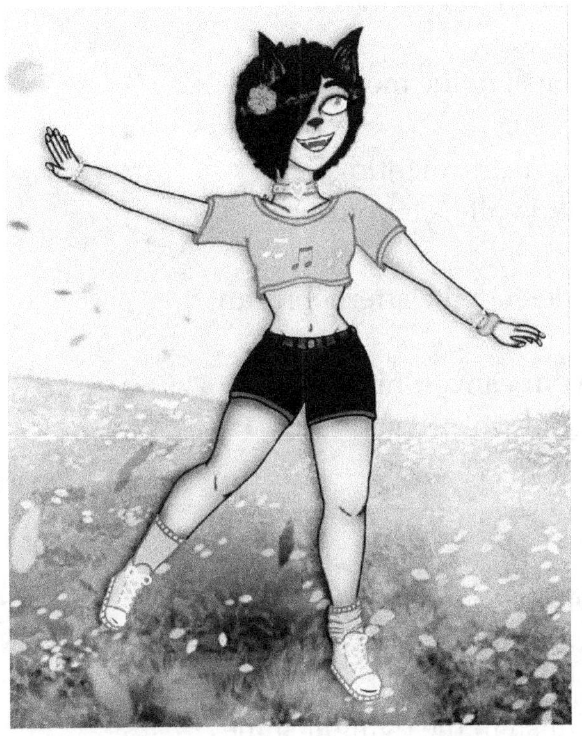

"Little Puppy Dog" By Tweetie

A Voiceless Nightingale

By Tweetie Snow

Hush, hush in the morning, dew.

Cry your tears, nightingale;
not a soul will hear your wail.

Hush, hush in the afternoon sun.

Paint your canvas, nightingale;
Not a soul will see your art.

Hush, hush in the evening glow.

Act your part, nightingale;
Not a soul will watch your play.

Hush, hush in the twilight shine.

Hold your love, nightingale;
Not a soul will love you back.

Sing, sing under the nightly stars.

It is too late for anyone to hear your voice.

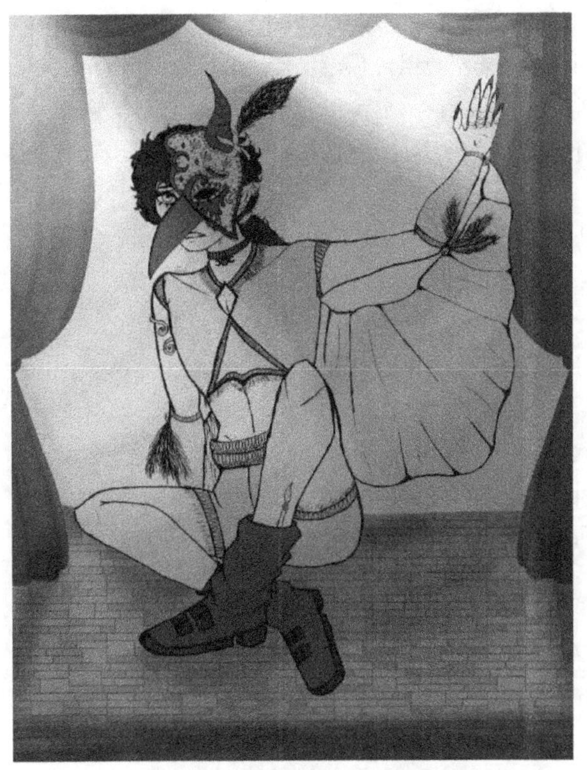

"Act Your Part, Nightingale" By Tweetie

A Courageous Kraken

By Tweetie Snow

The salt only burns open wounds, not scars.
Glorious sails torn but still flying with pride.
Sailors in the sea swim in Kraken's abattoirs,
Horrors of tendrils buried men in the dark tide.

Dawn's halo is a sailor's graceful savior.
Reverence for grotesque beasts of love.
Seas are no place for humorous behavior.
Yet, a Kraken still believes in Cupid above all else.

Courageous Kraken, find love in your peers.
Protect your oceans; leave the rocks to him.
Pure Fervor Sons, why must you be queers?
Courageous Kraken, loving a dragon's whim.

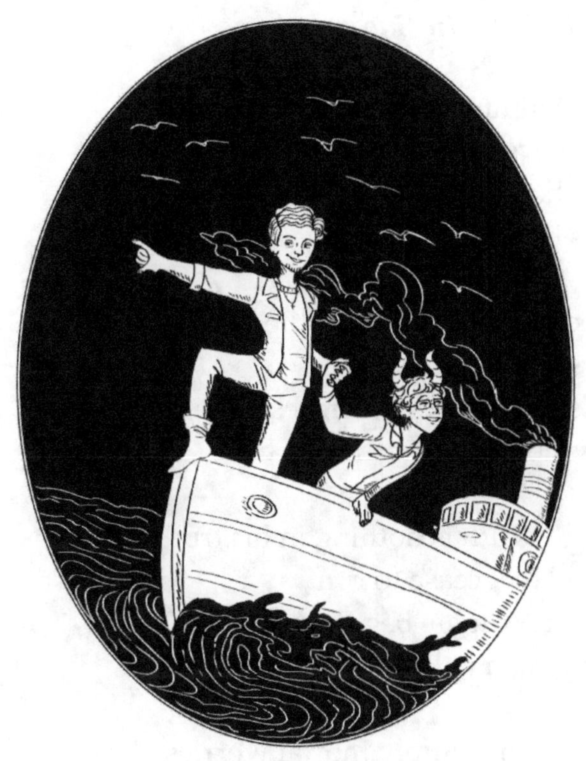

"A Kraken and His Dragon" By Anonymous

Scythe

By Tweetie Snow

Golden shimmers of watchful blades,
Eyes for eyes takes a life.
Forget the days that death forbids,
Sight is blind under his scythe.

Righteous and sinful fade the same,
Fingers ache as stories end.
Death strips glory and erases fame,
His scythe skin hands to the bone.

Earning wealth is nothing in his truth,
Legs and feet cease to run.
Hurt and Struggle beg for my youth,
Limping men will fall to their scythe.

Ideologies are simply mortal worries,
Lungs shrivel to hollow stone.
The cold skin exhales frozen flurries,
Breathless as his scythe strikes.

Dandelion

By Tweetie Snow

Pat! Pat! Pat!

I hear a little sparrow on an oak branch,
He hums the tunes of spring forenoons.

Chirp! Chirp! Chirp!

Dawning birds wake to give peaceful songs,
Dandelions wildly flourish in the fields.

Yellow, White, gone too soon.

The zenith of life is white rondure blooms,
Sow the seeds as you are reaped for wishes.

Pat! Pat! Pat!

Children's scurrying feet and hearty laughs,
A gush of breath begins the next spring.

A Vocal Phoenix

By Tweetie Snow

Love is a wild river of moss
on cold stones.
Love is a forest ablaze, trees
of burnt flesh.
Love is a storm ravaging
homes of all life.
Love is a fruitful garden,
lush and forbidden.

Mud on young skin stains
memories that claw for
freedom. Talons of new
hands scrape ways to relive
wistful friendships. Yet
stones remain unscratched.

Can a Phoenix play the part
of a boy? Can a boy become
a Phoenix, or is it what he's
always been?

Trees with hearts carved
with a knife, now ash of old
hope.
A beak of new calls sings
for the missing forgiveness.
So vocal yet unheard by
men.

Can a Phoenix call a boy his
friend?
Can a boy befriend a
Phoenix, or is it just a
hopeless delusion?

Clouds full of rolling
thunder frighten those
without shelter.
Feathers of wings cannot
withstand the wind and
rain.
Yet the Phoenix keeps
flying.

Can a Phoenix pray to a
god?
Can a god answer a vocal
bird's prayer, or will he
throw it in the furnace?

Fresh plums sparkle in the
noon fall so soon to ugly
rot.
The heart of a phoenix
desires the taste. Yet all
have rotten off the branches.

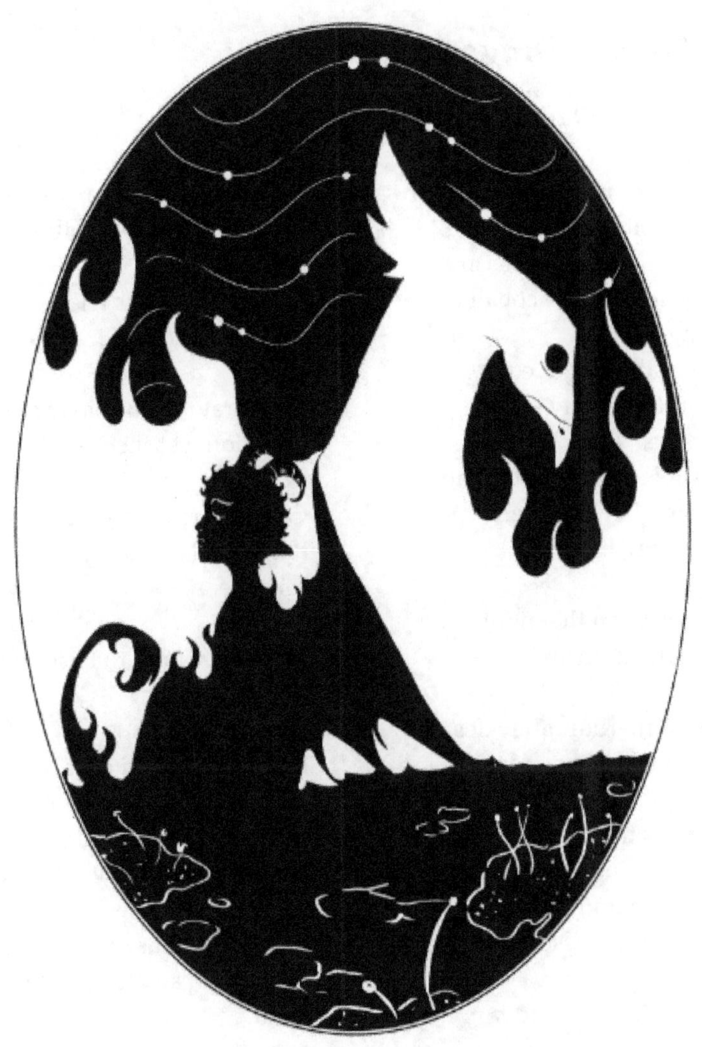

"Can A Phoenix Pray to a God?" By Anonymous Artist

A Solemn Dragon

By Tweetie Snow

I thought it was your face in
my habitual bitter coffee,
Your freckled cheeks are
rosy, and eyes a cobalt day
bringer.
Your soft ginger curls are
smirched in my eternal
reverie.
A smile like an effulgent
prism of every hue, a
gleaming lingers.

Mother, can the night sky
love the morrow?

A cummerbund buckles me
with your arms of lucid
gaiety.
Black is mundane until I see
my grieving livery today.
Your ignominy revealed
your abrupt rescale scent
mortality.
All smoldered under my
father's might, no time for
decay.

Father, can you forgive my
pitiful sorrow?

Necrosis is my strongest
proprium in my devilry
studies.
Yet, mourning is a leg
severed by a hot, ireful iron
blade.
Inveterate memorials are
tradition, yet they lack
priorities.
Carmine roses are not the
daffodils I wished yet father
forbade.

My love, I pray to be joining
you in Heaven.

Death is blinded eyes
stripped of sight by hot
carnal hands.
You are my crux of life, and
from here I cease hope.
Countless treasures, though
no hope in a gold wedding
band.
I am a solemn dragon
resting in his hoards to
cope.

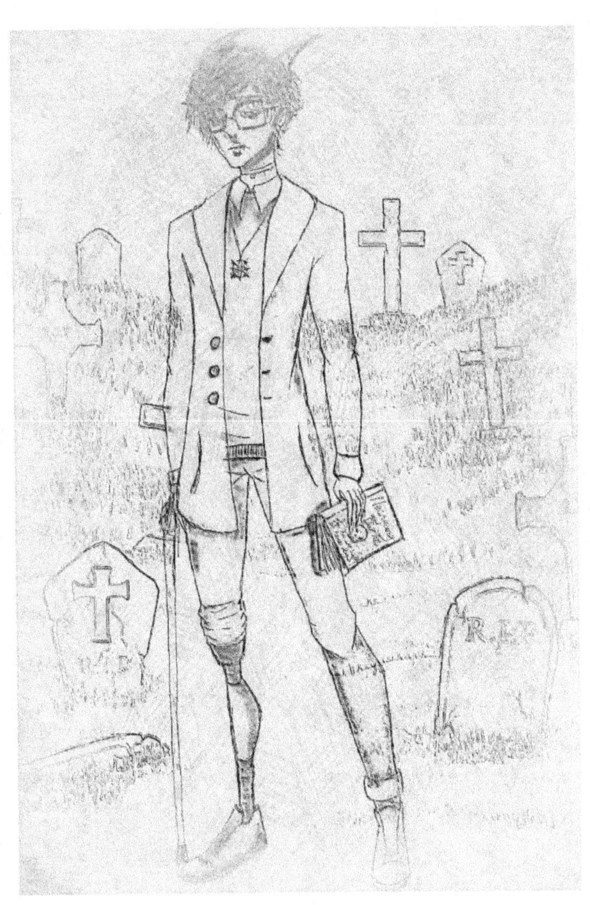

" A Solemn Dragon" By Tweetie Snow

Naomi Rose

By Tweetie Snow

My Naomi Rose,
Glimmering serenity,
In my rose garden.

My Naomi Rose,
Knives like thorns pierce her fair skin,
Roses curse my old heart.

My Naomi Rose,
A daughter of mine gone now,
Grieving her sweet song.

Lycandope Forest

By Tweetie Snow

Sanctuary home,
Evergreens and chilling springs;
Refuge for wolfmen.

Howl at the midnight,
Let our people hear our call;
Sounds of ancestors.

Tomorrow is new,
The canopy is tranquil,
I am at home.

The Alpha

By Tweetie Snow

They took my howl but not my spirit.
Against the martinet on the fields of blood,
From humble infancy to the highest merit,
They took my howl but not my spirit.
A Title is earned, not one you can inherit.
Born in the trenches, that rain does flood.
They took my howl but not my spirit,
Against the martinet on the fields of blood.

Lunageo

By Tweetie Snow

Name for lunar orb,
An island of pure white sand,
Country of magic.

A Golden palace,
Across from haggling markets,
Country of power.

In the rancid depths,
The mystic marsh forbidden,
Country of secrets.

Weather's Lullaby

By Tweetie Snow

The thunder is your drumline,
The rain is your soft chorus,
The wind plays a tune so fine,

My child, hear the melody.
Storms are gentle ensembles,
Fear not, weather's sweet elegy,

Sleep well, my thundercloud.

Quietem

By Tweetie Snow

Name for Quietness,
Order and obedience,
Country of edict.

Docks to evergreens,
A spectacle of beauty,
Country of array.

Fort to tenements,
Surviving stones of past reigns,
Country of decree.

Soleil

By Tweetie Snow

My soleil, your flesh is of golden Heaven,
Your eyes are of the dearest holy angels,
The sun shall not have any other labels.
Engulfs my heart into your possession,
Sweet nurture is your divine profession.
I am a humble bird balancing on cables,
My wings flutter for your soul, enables.
I bow to the goddess and thy succession.

You are my muse, my colored canvas,
Your hues are splattered on my pages.
I am your humble bird, singing to you,
To you, I lay weak and utterly anxious.
My dear goddess reign for endless ages,
As your nightingale, only to you, I coo.

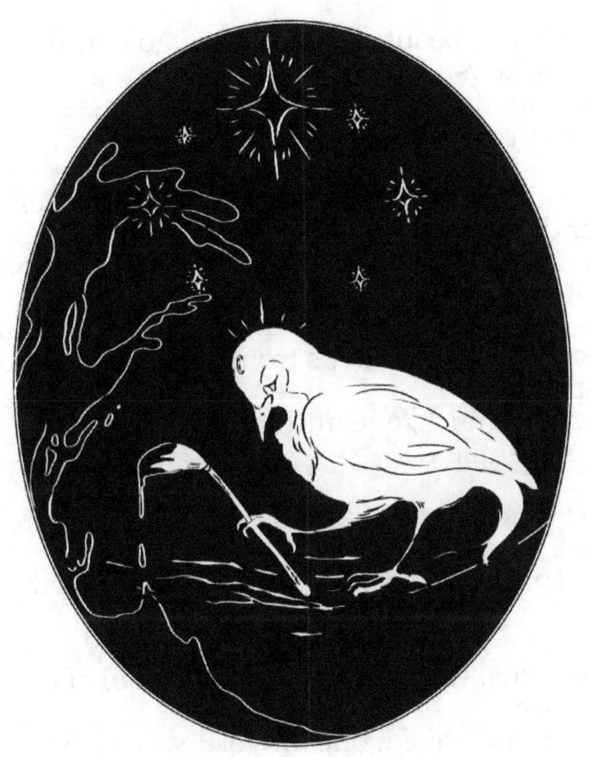

"Paint Your Canvas, Nightingale" by Anonymous

Dearest

By Tweetie Snow

Dearest Soliel, beauty is thy skin of golden stars and
truthful glitters.
I know I am dirty, one unworthy of a blessed
presence by you.

Dearest kitsune, sin is an act of thine, a body of
sinister desires.
I know I am filth, one unworthy of a holy temptress's
bow.

Dearest Kanin, small hops from thee create winds of
high speeds.
I know I am muck, one unworthy of a gentle
highness's smile.

Dearest thue'bahn, slither your ancient wisdom into
thy soul.
I know I am sick, one unworthy of the divine hand of
a prince.

Dearest Luna, wings of an angel and soul of demons
within thee.
I know I am damned, one unworthy of a false
goddess's kiss.

Dearest αρvi, horns of wicked curses thy heavenly
eyes.
I know I am rot, one unworthy of a fallen angel's
healing tears.

Dearest eagle, halos of mother's love shine above thy
head.
I know I am dead, one unworthy of witnessing
dearest gods.

Serpent at Sea

By Tweetie Snow

Shores of tiny grains curse my fatal gashes

Aboard my stolen coble; row, men, row

Embering wood on dry shores are ashes

Call out her name, the dearest calypso

She finds you unworthy, now sink below

A slithering thief knows no good honor

Thief now row a stiff; Oh, ocean goner

The twilight heavens are a swimmer's map

For Storm less skies, pray to the great Donar

Your serpent life ends to a thunderclap

Ribbons and Roses

By Tweetie Snow

Satin silk, a classy ribbon upon my ears,

Clipped, cut, and tied in a perfect bow.

White, red, all the color soon disappears.

Satin silk, a classy ribbon upon my ears,

Harsh black roses are awakening our fears.

Forgotten petals leave when the winds blow.

Satin silk, a classy ribbon upon my ears,

 Our story belongs to the ones we know.

Careless Beauty

By Tweetie Snow

Lovely emerald fox, what pleases you?
Is it the careless beauty of an unfit soul?
Is it the eyes of mystics lining anew?

Pretty emerald fox, what pleases you?
Is it the food above the embering coal?
Is it the men you so carelessly woo?

Fair emerald fox, what pleases you?
Do you even know what you stole?
Is it my heart or the hearts of a few?

Sightly emerald fox, what pleases you?
Is it the zealful women who pay a toll?
Is it the grass covered in morning dew?

Fine emerald fox, what pleases you?
I cannot find the answers to your droll.
You fill your heart with sex and stew.

Mystic emerald fox, what pleases you?
Dearest fox, you have all my control.
Oh, careless beauty, hold that as true.
I beg you, fox, tell me how to please you.

Heaven

By Tweetie Snow

Halos,
Gold feathered wings,
Beautiful regency,
Thy angels of the sweet heavens,
Pray now.

Lion,
on a gold throne.
Pearls in his many eyes,
benevolent and all-loving,
Pray now.

Angels,
Holy council,
Holding hands of mortals,
Fate, nature, mortality, woe,
Pray now.

The Angel of Providence

By Tweetie Snow

Stood in the hall of God, in the spirit of good fate. To you, to all, I am the man whom all men fear to come.

Holy fate, holy light; let no halo shatter under the sins of man.

Sitting on the throne of eternity, rightfully sat upon weak divinity. To you, to all, I am the angel of all that may come.

Holy fate, holy night; let all fallen burn in the 8 torturous halls of Hell.

Kneeling to no other, as I am above all, there is and ever was. To you, to all, I am God, and to this world I came.

The Angel of Piety

By Tweetie Snow

Sacred lands are trampled by damned feet in clambering boots of steel.

Oaks to grains of sand, dry soiled lands send cracks in a glass seal.

To God, we pray for mercy and wonder.

Gold is no worthier than soot scuffed on a disdainful man's heel.

Despite all the warnings, I have yet to see an iron elephant kneel.

The Angel of Evocation

By Tweetie Snow

Who are you, if not, who you have been?
Where are you, if not home in bed?
What are you, if not your closest Kin?
When are you going in your head?

I am who I have been.
I am at home in bed.
I am like my closest Kin.
I am stuck in my head.

Reflect on the ones loved and lost,
Recapture the wonders of yesterday,
Recall the lives lived at all costs.

Who are you? If not, who will you be?
Where are you? If not, where are you going?
What are you if not what you maybe?
When are you going as time is flowing?

I will be who I will be,
I will be where I am going,
I will be what I may be,
I will be going as time is flowing.

Reminisce the thoughts of recognition,
Remember the delusions of yesterday,
Reconnect in thy evocation.

The Angel of Viability

By Tweetie Snow

Oh, Melancholy!

Vines of nurture grow wild woes,

Oh, Father Nature!

The Angel of Fluidity

By Tweetie Snow

Flow is temptation.

Rivers glitter from the lies,

Fluid and untrue.

The Angel of Luminescence

By Tweetie Snow

A stinging warmth blind,

Vanity is the sunshine,

Orbs of ugly glow.

The Angel of Mortality

By Tweetie Snow

The divine fury of angels is ponderous,
upon the misty fields of sleeping ewes.
Pure young sheep will die soon, softly and
nonporous,
Yet not without purpose, for she is you.

Your brothers gave you a shepherd's hook to beguile,
You harvest the departed as your herd.
Mortals tremble at your expected arrival,
Though you are loving, kind, and undeterred.

A temptress mortal seduced your poor, watchful eyes,
She stripped you of blessed virginity.
An angel does not bleed or meet his poor demise.
Your brothers will strip you of dignity.

Dear angel, with horns of a ram and falcon wings,
Why did you fall from the heavens above?
I send you my sad prayer for the queens and kings,
Send us your son, tender angel of love.

The Angel of Ardency

By Tweetie Snow

Oh, no

Sweet Cupid,

My lover is long gone;

Infatuated with a rose.

Tears fell,

Fell far.

Sweet Eros,

My love is gravely ill;

Plagued with hatred.

I beg,

Beg you.

Philokrates,

Heal my lover of all her woes;

Kill ardency,

For her.

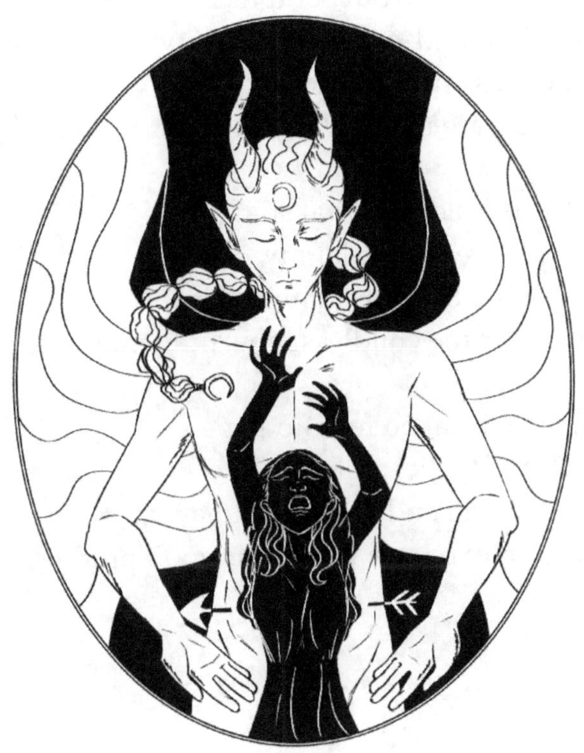

"Kill Ardency" By Anonymous Artist

The Angel of Woe

By Tweetie Snow

You are much like your seraphic brothers.
They are light and righteous divinity.
You are chaos and tenebrosity.
In truth, you are not the holy others.

Under the rubble, a mortal smother.
A third eye oversees calamity.
You watch the humans' inhumanity.
Shed tears for the childless mourning mothers.

Now, an eye is taken for another's
On the eve of the insanity,
Your scythe will end wicked humanity.
Soon, you may be one with your good brothers.

Hell

By Tweetie Snow

Eight proud
Kingdoms of Sin
Sit on the scorching hill,
Under our darkest past mistakes,
Pray now.

Sinners
Are not exempt
From the Gray demon kings.
Do not let your gross sins fester,
Pray now.

Disdain,
Proclivity,
Vexation, Voracince,
Theurgy, greed, and Begrudgement.
Pray now.

The King of Disdain

By Tweetie Snow

Did my deeds injure your fragile pride?
Identity of a son is all but celebrated,
Sin and voice, all my disdain debated.
Damnation is not my fate; it is my bride.
A father and son, a soldier and king,
I present a bushel, what will you bring?
New creation is not avenging; one still died.

A man and a god,
Divine son of an angel.
A man and a devil,
Men have no chance of survival.

Perched on your throne, above all,
Real kings would lay among the sick.
Indignation is a liar's crown's fall,
Dying is mercy from Hell's hot pick.
Endings are rarely triumphant.

The King of Vexation

By Tweetie Snow

Vain
Evil
Xebec
Arsenal
Treacherous
Ignited
Oxidize
Settlement

Retched war burns good men.
Hurt in the wage of battle,
Yearning for the safety of home,
Snakes hid among your brothers.

War
Rage
Ambition
Temperament
Honor

The King of Proclivity

By Tweetie Snow

Protect me from the hands of barbarity,
Ridged hands glide across my skin.
Oh, please, Father, save me from Hell!
Clinging to your feet from salacity,
Liveliness fades to wicked sleep.
I dream of the horrors of the enslaved,
Villainous men grasping with proclivity.
I no longer desire. I only fear him.
To be innocent again, youth is mortal.
You did not protect me from atrocity.

Am I still pure, or am I ruined?
May my soul be cleansed, or am I filthy?
Am I worthy to forgive in a defiled body?
Repent for my detestable sins of desire,
Are you listening or am I now all alone?

Lust breaks the bright, pellucid virgin,
Undiluted faith is a child's deportment.
Suffering under the watchful eyes of men,
To be filled with hope again is contentment.

The king of Avarice

By Tweetie Snow

An urge for more than little,
Vile acts to obtain simple grains,
Actions that turn soft to brittle.
Retributions for your eager pains,
Ignoring duties is not an acquittal.
Carving coins is a lifetime of chains,
Everyone's greed will grow and belittle.

Earning is a man's honorable work.
Search, I beg thee, for honest labor,
Hanging, who steals from the clerk.
Avarice is not a helpful neighbor,
Raiders and tax collectors are murk.

Greedy fingers pay no tributes.
Racing the wicked is restless,
Everyone prays to whoever constitutes.
Ejaculation for the penniless,
Desires are dangerous attributes.

The King of Voracince

By Tweetie Snow

Vicious cravings arise in sin.
Obsession drives a man to murder.
Ravaging hunger drives a man to eat.
Aching guilt drives a man to starvation.
Consuming too much in life is death.
Ingest truth, not human consumption.
Nibble just a bit becomes a large bite,
Craving is such a dangerous game;
Ecstasy in temporary frenzy.

My stomach grows limitless for the yearning,
An apple is just an apple until there are ten.
Contain your feasting, or you shall suffer,
Eating so lasciviously is killing you.

Gormandize thy wants,
Longing thy true indulgences.
Urging for more self-riches,
Thirst for the waters of mania.
To eat thy desires,
Outcry in depravity.
Nature knows a balance,
Yearning for freedom.

The King of Faineance

By Tweetie Snow

Fairness is a joke of naive fools in life trifles,
A man is not a man if he sits to wait for work.
I am the devil of the home; in your bed, I lurk.
No devil has time to judge in a sinner's trials,
Endings are slow in a fool's pointless story.
Apathy is the way of a devil, a virtue in the core,
Newborns are no exception to judgment.
Closure is for the race's swift and shrewd,
Equity of torpid souls is early damnation.

Slow and dilatory like the men of the land,
Lingering on dirt with an undivine hand.
Obsessions with negligence are damned,
The laggard will rot with the gluttonous.
Hasty will beat the belated burning of greed.

The King of Begrudgement

By Tweetie Snow

Son, will you not desire what is not yours?
I have many plums, yet you beg for apples.
If I grow apples, you beg for plums,
If I pick plums, you desire apples.
What is it that you wish to change, my son?

Petite, delicate fruits, purple and sweet,
Indignantly, you refuse my labors of love?
If I collect roses, you beg for daisies,
If I gather daisies, you desire roses.
Begrudging son, what will please you?

Swirling red wonders of garden's envy,
Infuriatingly greedy you are to me, my son.
If I give you coins, you beg for gifts.
If I present you with gifts, you desire coins.
Providing you plenty, yet you are so needy.

The King of Theurgy

By Tweetie Snow

Across a temple, I hold the awakening like a mother,
Hear me, dearest, do you fancy a spell?
Of snakes and birds, who would eat who before the
other?
Answer my loving riddle, dearest nightingale.

In your visions, do you see me beside you,
A crown upon our heads, a halo in our souls?
Tell me, can our allurement enchant more than a few?
Dearest stag, you are my augury of coals.

Dearest daughter, coo like a dove or hiss like a snake,
A crown is just gold without your little white brow.
The throne is soft, and the bones are all but fake.
Dearest dove, answer my loving fatherly vow.

I am king, and with the strength of theurgy, you will
be my answer.

Forgive Me

By Tweetie Snow

I am the spirit of blame,
Tip the bottle to my lips to sip solid poisons.
Obstructing the trust of familial honor.

Kneeling before you for exoneration,
Kneeling before you for vindication,
Kneeling before you for exculpation,

Forgive my mind, dearest family.

This is my plea of blame,
Served my imprisonment in horrid walls,
Begging that my crimes are acquittal.

Kneeling before you for amelioration,
Kneeling before you for palliation,
Kneeling before you for reparation,

Forgive my soul, dearest family.

To My Momma

By Tweetie Snow

From the hands of Heaven to your arms of grace, I am
yours.
Shaped in the mold of your model, crafted in your
care.
Though I am not you, I am a piece of your creation.

From tweeting bird themes to college degrees, I am
yours.
Following beside, hand in hand, the treacherous road
is yet to end.
Though I am not you, I am with you in honest
conviction.

From horrid nightmares to sappy movies, I am yours.
Always within reach, next door in your time of need
Though I am not you, I will care for you with
maternal compassion.

From tears in the night to filled shopping carts, you
are mine.
I am your eldest daughter, and you my caring
mother,
Though we are not each other, our love will meet no
desolation.

Tails of Pontoons

By Tweetie Snow

Waves of our creation are tails of pontoons,
The fish do greet me with simple bliss,
As I love the salient blue ocean mist.

I see a man, hair as gray as a storm cloud,
Sit upon the deck with a rod and hook,
A chuckle, a huff, with his holy book,
Evocating small youthful pleasures allowed.

Fantasize a grand marlin or a small carp,
no mind to size only to the heart of fish.
One more day on the water is all I wish.

We may catch a ton or perhaps just none.
I am a wave behind his humble fishing boat.
My mother now me, we both stay afloat.
My grandfather is my pontoon in the sun.

To My Little Sister

By Tweetie Snow

Began in the midst of a late evening dinner prayer,
Bring me an angel with green eyes and golden hair.
Blessed with a princess from Heaven's holy arms.

Sweet little sister Ghi, you live with timeless care.
Staying small and innocent for an old life is not fair.
Swimming as a mermaid with many mystic charms.

Wishing you all the loving best as you grow each year,
Writing our story with all my blessed older sister flare,
Waiting behind you with all my might at all alarms.

To think, all this goodness came from a single prayer.

My Daemon

By Tweetie Snow

Howl, hoot, huff, and holler!

Kindly bow to the Daemon of twisted twine,
Restraining frail figurines dancing dashingly.

White, wit, wail, and whimper!

Dazzle me, Daemon, I plea for pleasantries.
Chuckling, chortling, with a wantoned wolf.

Serph, serpent, sense, and seller!

Write me luring lyrics, dearest Daemon.
Ballad balance, an angry angel's anguish.

Moon, move, monture, and molar!

Demolish despicable durability, my Daemon.
Break brittle brothel relationships of mine.

Daemon, demon, damned, and demolisher!

Many envies even may my damned Daemon.
Soft sleep of restful resistance is your tomb.

Love, longing, loss, and lower!

To Queen Eloise

By Tweetie Snow

What does a royal crown mean to you, Queen Eloise?
Is it the regency of beauty or perhaps a severed head?
I have oathed to your throne and paid all your fees.
I would lay awake in hopes you emerge from bed.

Why did you throw me in the dungeon, Queen
Eloise?
Am I not your purest white rabbit with a broken
clock?
I have fallen into your hole of despair and swam teary
seas.
My dolor heart is far too big to open such a tiny lock.

When shall they be off with my capitulum, Queen
Eloise?
Shall I wear a white rose on my lapel to paint red?
Spill my blood, I may smile as wide draped in lunacy.
Oh, Queen Eloise, how could you wish me dead?

This is Not A Poem

By Tweetie Snow

This is not a poem; it is a plea.
Reflect on your old actions,
Forgive your imperfections,
Mourn woeful confrontations,
Listen not to the man behind the wheel.

This is not a poem; it is an apology.
Sorry for my damn poor choices.
Sorry for the lies I told.
Sorry for my words of hate.
Listen not to the man behind the desk.

This is not a poem; it is an eulogy.
We have lost a naive child.
We have lost a timid tween.
We have lost an eager teen.
Listen not to the man behind the voice.

This is not a poem; this is my reality.